# FINE ART QUILTS

## Work by Artists of the
## Contemporary QuiltArt Association

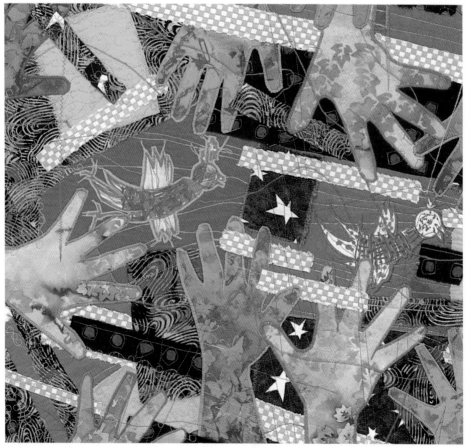

Detail of *A Bird in the Hand* by Maude May

FIBER
STUDIO
PRESS

## ACKNOWLEDGMENTS

A special thank you to CQA members Stephanie Randall Cooper, Gretchen Echols, Jean Koskie, Karen Perrine, and Kelli Radcliffe for their exceptional efforts and dedication over the years.

We want to give particular recognition to Cale Kinney, formerly of Foster/White Gallery, Kirkland, Washington; Rick Gottas, owner of American Art Company, Tacoma, Washington; Sharon Ducey, Director of Exhibitions at the Washington State Convention Center, Seattle, Washington; and Peggy Weiss, Curator of the Seafirst Gallery, Seattle; for their public encouragement and support of our artists and their work.

Our appreciation to Laura M. Reinstatler, Kathryn Ezell, and Fiber Studio Press for their belief in our organization and in the importance of the art quilt.

We are grateful to the families of CQA members for their "behind the scenes" support of our work.

We thank all the sponsors of our tenth-anniversary celebration, especially: Alaska Dyeworks, American & Efird Inc., American Quilter Magazine/AQS, Bernina of America, Inc., Coats & Clark, Cotton Club, Hobbs Bonded Fibers, Hoffman Fabrics, Husqvarna Viking Sewing Machine Co., In The Beginning Fabrics, P&B Textiles, Pfaff American Sales Corp., Rowenta, the Seattle foundation, South Sea Imports, Testfabrics, and V.I.P. Fabric Co.

## DEDICATION

To all CQA members past and present, and to Sharon Yenter of In The Beginning Fabrics, thank you for your years of dedication, commitment, and support.

## CREDITS

Editor-in-Chief . . . . . . . . . . Kerry I. Smith
Technical Editor . . Laura M. Reinstatler
Managing Editor . . . . . . . . . . Judy Petry
Copy Editor . . . . . . . . . . . . . . Tina Cook
Proofreader . . . . . . . . . . . . Leslie Phillips
Design Director . . . . . . Cheryl Stevenson
Text and Cover Designer . . . Kay Green
Editorial Assistant . . . . . . . . Kathryn Ezell
Production Assistant . . Marijane E. Figg
Photographer . . . . . . . . . . . Brent Kane

**Library of Congress Cataloging-in-Publication Data**

Fine art quilts : works by artists of the Contemporary QuiltArt Association.
  p. cm.
  Exhibition catalog.
  ISBN 1-56477-193-8
  1. Quilts—United States—History—20th century—Exhibitions.
  2. Contemporary QuiltArt Association—Membership—Exhibitions.
  I. Contemporary QuiltArt Association.
NK9112.F47 1997
746.46' 0973' 074797772—dc21          97-16857
                                                                CIP

FIBER
STUDIO
PRESS

Fine Art Quilts: Work by Artists of the Contemporary QuiltArt Association

©1997 by That Patchwork Place, Inc.
That Patchwork Place, Inc.
PO Box 118
Bothell, WA 98041-0118 USA

Printed in Hong Kong
02 01 00 99 98 97     6 5 4 3 2 1

## MISSION STATEMENT

*We are dedicated to providing quality products and service by working together to inspire creativity and to enrich the lives we touch.*

# TABLE OF CONTENTS

(Top) Detail of *Faces II*
by Elizabeth Hendricks

(Middle) Detail of *At the
Temple of the Queen
of Pineapple* by Pia Fish

(Bottom) Detail of *Firstborn*
by Sally A. Sellers
Photo by Bill Bachhuber

# INTRODUCTION

Until recently, most of us thought of a bed covering when we heard the term *quilt*. Usually this image was of a utilitarian household furnishing, handmade, with two or more colors pieced into blocks or appliquéd in floral designs.

The first era of the quilt's popularity began as settlers of the New World sewed together every scrap of available fabric to keep their families warm. Many beds displayed at least one quilt, and some fortunate family members slept under several. Over the years, utilitarian quilts became inspirations for more decorative quilts, used not only to provide warmth but also to express aesthetic ideas, brightening their makers' homes. As a quilt survived decades of use, the descendants of its maker added new quilts to their collection. Quiltmaking became a means of communication, of connection, of sharing. Quilts play important roles in family histories: documented wedding quilts, memory quilts, commemorative quilts, and friendship or album quilts appear frequently in historical records and journals.

In 1971 Jonathan Holstein curated an exhibit of quilts for the Whitney Modern Art Museum in New York City. This exhibition, entitled *Abstract Design in American Quilts*, proved a catalyst for the public, especially for quiltmakers and artists, who viewed the quilt differently after the exhibition. Interest in the historical quilt and in the quilt as a medium for innovative expression began the

exponential growth quiltmaking has experienced over the past twenty-five years.

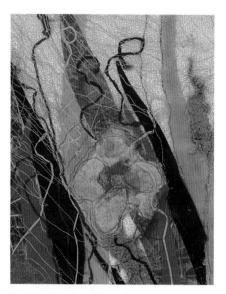

Detail of *Summer's Gold*
by Carla DiPietro

As interest in quiltmaking renewed and grew, certain tenets of the craft changed. Quiltmakers began to make quilts of all sizes and for all purposes, from king-size bed coverings to small wall hangings to works in miniature so tiny they seem to defy what is humanly possible. Color relationships and the rhythmic and graphic qualities of traditional patterns attracted the interest of fiber artists, who also appreciated the textural aspects of quilting that added to the works' visual impact. Stretching the boundaries of quiltmaking through nontraditional piecing and appliqué techniques led these innovators in directions that

excited increasing numbers of artists of all media. Within a short time, artists began creating work that included paint, embellishments, and found objects; nontraditional materials, such as metals and plastics; and surface manipulations such that some of the pieces barely resembled quilts at all. Now quilts of all sizes and styles are often displayed like precious remnants of ancient textiles, never having been considered as bed covers.

Today, artists who make innovative quilts do not always work from a foundation of traditional quiltmaking techniques or styles. Many train as painters, sculptors, or ceramists but choose quilts as their medium. Their quilts not only express eye-pleasing interactions of color and design, but also include intellectual explorations of design elements and social or political observations (although quiltmakers throughout history have devoted their efforts within more formal parameters to any of these aspects).

Only within the past few years has the work of a handful of fiber artists and quiltmakers begun to be accepted into prestigious exhibitions, museums, and galleries. Having roots in "women's work," fiber pieces—especially quilts, with their associations as functional objects—are considered, and even discounted, as craft instead of fine art. The struggle to be accepted in the fine-art arena is waged every time a quilt is entered in and rejected from an art exhibition.

Artists engaged in this conflict are seeking ways to eliminate prejudice. They have put together shows, exhibition tours, organizations, and symposia to educate the public (and themselves) and to change the perceptions of the quilt as *women's* art. Through diligent efforts, their work—the quilt—in all its forms, is gaining acceptance as a serious medium.

The Contemporary QuiltArt Association formed in 1987 as a Puget Sound regional group interested in sharing ideas and techniques for creating innovative quilts. Its members have worked diligently for ten years to educate themselves and the public about the quilt's place in the fine-art realm. Throughout the pages of this book, the artists' works speak articulately to CQA's directives. Some work borrows heavily from traditions of the past; some work moves into areas that may stretch the definitions of quilt-related art. A most remarkable feature of the organization is that its members' work represents diverse styles and sensibilities. Each piece reflects careful thought and commitment to the artist's personal journey and documents her locus on that continuum. This catalog of work testifies to the dynamic growth that the Contemporary QuiltArt Association fosters and the degree to which each member assumes personal responsibility to contribute to it.

Detail of *Flapdoodle* by Terri Shinn

Detail of *Latticeworks III* by Carol Roi Olsen

# HISTORY

By Gretchen Echols

## MISSION STATEMENT

*The Contemporary QuiltArt Association (CQA) is an arts organization which sponsors and promotes the professional endeavors of artists working in the quilt medium. The association seeks to educate the public about this art form.*

The Contemporary QuiltArt Association has grown gradually over the years, achieving its present form through the efforts, strengths, and ideas of its members. It began with a series of lectures and has progressed from shows in small community galleries to exhibitions attracting thousands. The continued efforts of its members has secured the Contemporary QuiltArt Association a presence in both local and national art scenes.

The group evolved out of a four-part lecture series organized by Sharon Yenter, owner of In The Beginning Fabrics in Seattle, and Lorraine Torrence, during the spring of 1986. Four regional fiber artists showed slides of their work and discussed issues faced by textile artists. The lecture audience, united by their interest in the art quilt and their delight in the discussions, decided to meet on a monthly basis.

The participants visualized an organization that would support art quilts and their makers. Originally called the Northwest Association of Quilt Artists, the group elected their first president and met informally for more than a year. The group studied artists working in many media, discussed the business of being an artist, created ways to exhibit their work, and developed a network of fiber artists.

Early in 1988 a formal structure emerged. The group established dues, chose a logo, elected officers, and changed its name to the Contemporary Quilt Association. The association focused on supporting each other's artistic efforts and on educating the public about the quilt as fine art.

While working on bylaws, the group decided to create a nonprofit organization. The advantages were eligibility for grants and tax deductible donations as well as lower fees for meeting locations. The 501C-3 status, applied for in 1989, was provisionally granted in 1992. Proof that the organization is meeting the code requirements will eventually make the status permanent.

The group believed it was important to inform the public about the art quilt as well as to exhibit work personally. After shows in community galleries and an important exhibit at the Foster-White Gallery in Seattle, an opportunity for greater exposure arose. In 1991 the Seattle Center Folklife Festival was the setting for *By Design: The Quilt as Art*, which gave a large audience a chance to view art normally seen only in a gallery setting. Members displayed their art quilts and artist statements next to antique quilts selected from Sharon Yenter's collection. The artists practiced discussing their work to prepare themselves for questions from the public. The group wanted to describe the evolution of antique traditional works into art quilts and the concerns held in common by quiltmakers one hundred years ago and artists today.

In 1993 the group changed its name to the Contemporary QuiltArt Association (CQA) to better reflect its focus on fine art, and it selected a new, professionally designed logo that reflected the growth of individual expression out of traditional quiltmaking.

Since then, CQA has organized additional group shows and educational opportunities in various venues, most notably the 1994 *New Work: Makers, Methods, Meanings* show at the Washington State Convention and Trade Center in Seattle. The installation featured an Education Wall and a self-led Education Guide. Docent-led tours of the exhibit were offered for adults and children, and a curriculum guide, *Skills from School in Art*, provided teachers with lesson plans, for all grade levels, based on the art quilts in the show.

In 1995 *Non-Stop Northwest* was installed at the American Museum of Quilts and Textiles, San Jose, California, and in June 1997 the group mounted *On the Edge: Northwest*

*Quilt Art* at the Museum of the American Quilter's Society in Paducah, Kentucky.

To further educate CQA members, a program follows the business portion of each monthly Saturday meeting. Presentations are given by members, artists working in various media, and business professionals from the art community. A monthly newsletter reports on the activities of the group and features a listing of exhibition opportunities gleaned from various art magazines, tailored to the needs of the group.

About half the meeting is devoted to Showcase, when members exhibit and discuss current work. The members selected the term *Showcase* carefully, preferring it to "show and tell." Each quilt is hung on a wall, and the artist presents her intent for the piece. She might share any problems or successes encountered and request feedback. The goal is to provide a safe environment for public discussion and an opportunity to give thoughtful feedback about the art of others. Occasionally art professors present critiquing sessions to familiarize the membership with methods of and vocabulary for discussing art. The group has focused on artmaking issues rather than on technique-driven classes, which are already presented well at local shops and conferences.

While building the group structure, the artists also exhibited work individually, entering prestigious shows such as *Quilt National* in Athens, Ohio, and *Visions: Quilt San Diego*. Today, a high percentage of the membership is nationally known, and their work is consistently accepted into prominent shows, indicating the sophistication and professionalism of the group.

In recent years, fundraising has become an important part of CQA's efforts to support ambitious projects. The association has sought and received grants from local and state agencies and has encouraged member donations.

One individual's dedication to the group established the Sharon Pelton Memorial Fund. Sharon, an early member, discovered she had a terminal illness and wanted memorial donations to go to CQA. Eventually these donations were designated the Sharon Pelton Memorial Fund and kept separate from the operating funds. The memorial fund provides seed money, enabling special projects to get off the ground while additional funding is being sought. Occasionally the Board makes outright grants to a group project. The association's 1993 symposium (its first), *Difference: Fuel for Creation*, and many of the association's major projects, have directly benefited from the memorial fund's moneys. Recently CQA sold raffle tickets for two separate series of small art quilts (see pages 8–9). Each set of small works gives the winner an opportunity to own original artwork, and the proceeds go into the Sharon Pelton Memorial Fund.

Throughout 1997 CQA plans a minimum of ten events—one of which is this catalog—commemorating its tenth anniversary. The energy, creativity, and commitment of the association's membership cannot be understated. As colleagues at different stages in their journeys as artists, they have exchanged ideas, supported each other, and challenged themselves to think deeply about their art and to take risks to present it to the public.

The members of the Contemporary QuiltArt Association have created the exposure and educational opportunities necessary to build understanding of the quilt as a fine-art form. The group's national recognition and its dedicated and respected membership speak well for the success of the association's mission.

Detail of *Kuba III* by Elizabeth Ford-Ortiz

# SERIES QUILTS

Series quilts serve as vehicles both for raising money and for teaching about the art quilt. Each series consists of small, fully finished art quilts fastened to a single background. The series is raffled as a whole, and the winner can exhibit the small quilts singly or in one or more groups.

Each of the participating artists is given finished dimensions for one artwork. For the first series, participants were required to make a 15" x 15" piece and to use both black and white fabrics; the second series enlarged each piece to 18" x 18". Each participant writes an artist's statement, which is given to the winner of the quilt.

The first series was won by CQA member Carol Castaldi. The second-series winner will be announced at the end of 1997.

## Suite of Nine, 1995 (left)

*From left to right:*
First row: *Tiny Bubbles* by Elizabeth Ford-Ortiz, *Fat on Trial* by Grechen Echols, *Night Shift* by Louise Harris; second row: *Hard* by Elizabeth Hendricks, *Bertha's Blessing* by Margaret Ann Liston, *Only You* by Donna Prichard; third row: *Winter's Mysteries* by Carla DePietro, *Scene* by Janet Steadman, *Turtle* by Mia Rozmyn.

## Suite of Ten, 1997 (facing page)

*From left to right:*
First row: *Celebration* by Debra Calkins, *Celebrating the Sun* by Marlene Kissler; second row: *Celebrate!* by Karen Perrrine, *Euphrasies* by Maria Groat, *A Window of Opportunity* by Nancy Forrest; third row: *Kobe Lights* by Melody Crust, *Higher n' a Kite* by Helen L. Thompson, *Emergence* by Karen N. Soma; fourth row: *Celebrations: The Return of the Sun* by Gayle Bryan, *Celebrate X* by Erika Carter.

### *Meg Blau*

### (Mo)Thoughts Are Attracted to the Light; (Butterf)Lies Are Not

1992, 29" x 51"
Seattle, Washington

Through the metaphors of moths and butterflies, this piece celebrates light and the seeking of light. Moths, although night creatures, are so attracted to light they will do anything to get to it. Butterflies, on the other hand, live in the light, and seem to pay no attention to it. I used moths and butterflies to represent the conflict between ideas and lies. Ideas (or thoughts) constantly seek, and will try anything, to reach the light within my human spirit, while I try to keep ideas that are seeking light in the dark by telling myself lies.

For each background square, I first machine pieced a Double Wedding Ring square, then cut it into a new, smaller square. I assembled the resulting squares into Robbing-Peter-to-Pay-Paul squares. After assembling the background, I hand-appliquéd the butterflies and moths.

This is the second quilt in a series based on tropical rain forests. If you come close, you might hear the water rushing and the frogs croaking. Be aware, a cat is watching you!

Ten years ago, I spent time in a Central American jungle. After a long hike up a steamy river, we came to a waterfall, which seemed like heaven on earth. Back in the real world now, I work toward my personal destination of a career in tropical horticulture, while stitching the visions of rain forests that dance in my head. I want to thank Erika Carter for leading me up this particular path.

**Giselle Gilson Blythe**

Destination

1996, 40" x 47"
Seattle, Washington

**Rachel Brumer**

She Dressed with Care

1996, 60" x 63"
Seattle, Washington

This is one of five pieces in which I used the image of a hoop skirt. Colored patches line up over parts of the original print. Rather than restricting and confining movement and emotion, these hoops are expressive and mobile.

This piece explores the idea of the body as a map. The patches on the dress are significant and insignificant events, which can be decoded with the key of incidents running down the left side.

**Rachel Brumer**

Peach Pit, Washington

1996, 58" x 55"
Seattle, Washington

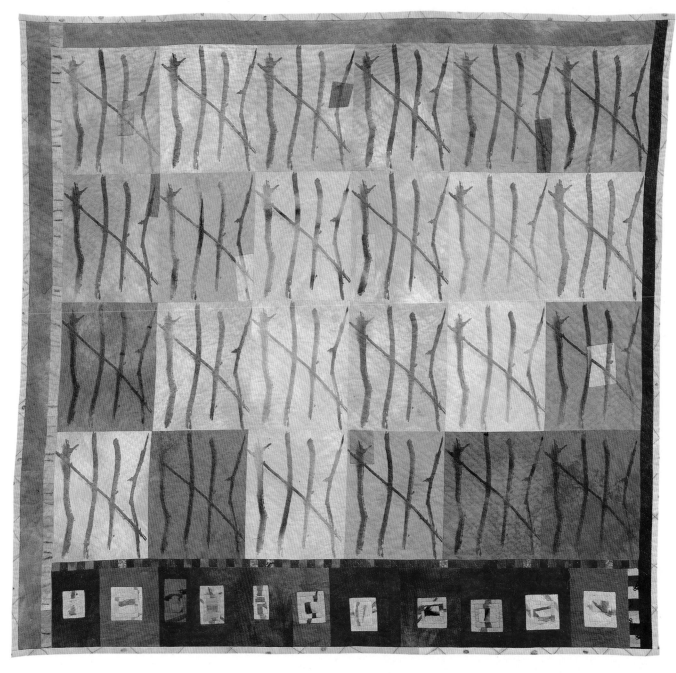

**Rachel Brumer**

120 +

1996, 60" x 58"
Seattle, Washington

I find I plot my time in small increments. This planning, to the minutiae, can be excruciating. I used sticks to represent an organic way of tracking time.

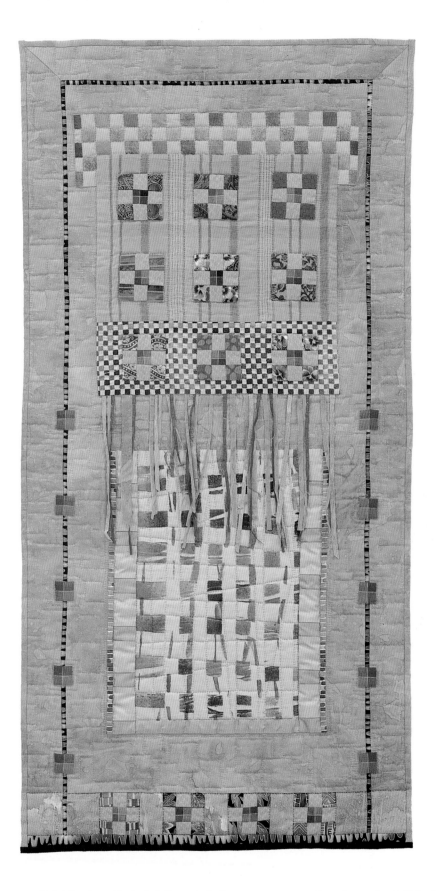

Paint it, piece it, stretch it, or slash it; start with a simple square and you can travel anywhere. Ideas evolve in the same way—forming, changing, and entering the world on their own terms.

**Gayle Bryan**

Point of Departure

1996, 20³/₄" x 41¹/₄"
Bellevue, Washington

### *Gayle Bryan*

## Prayers from Ancient Altars

1995, 115" x 45"
Bellevue, Washington

Several years ago, at a sacred spot on the grounds of Chartres Cathedral, I contemplated events that might have occurred there in centruies past. As I considered the generations of worshippers whose footsteps are covered by their descendants', the following images came to mind.

On a low hill where a brook once overflowed a tumble of rock, ancient people built an altar to celebrate the life-giving water and the return of spring. Through the years, many generations continued to gather at the stream, eventually renaming the time-honored goddesses and gods. On the old peoples' sacred site, descendants built a small chapel. When, in later years, that chapel crumbled, other worshipers cut stone and, atop the old foundation, built a glorious new cathedral. The people continued to celebrate the coming of spring but had long since forgotten the waters flowing beneath their floors.

People still come to the cathedral, trying to imagine the devotion that built it, awed by the statues, the colored glass, and the god they exalt. In a new language they speak the old prayers.

Without referring to a particular religion, *Prayers from Ancient Altars* layers images of faith and devotion, beginning with simple forms that could have been carved from stone or painted on monuments. Other, more complicated shapes are appliquéd with gilded fabrics, some overpainted to suggest the patina of centuries of incense.

Detail of *Prayers from Ancient Altars*

Detail of *Prayers from Ancient Altars*

**Gayle Bryan**

Rain (Garden Icon series)

1996, 12" x 24¼"
Bellevue, Washington

The world is different in the rain. In the mist, light changes, distances blur, colors soften, and vision muffles at the edges.

In rain's wake, streams fill and grass begins to grow, creating nourishment for the future.

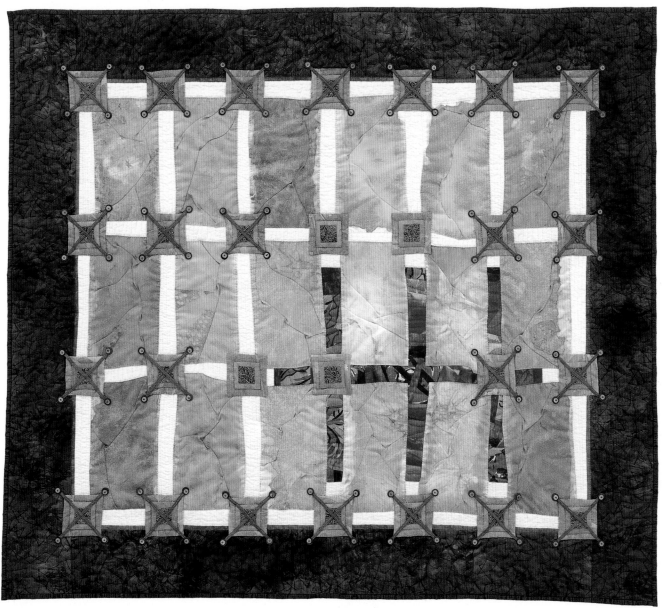

Just as we protect physical wounds with bandages, we also build armor around our emotional vulnerabilities. But that layer of protection can also bring isolation and stunted growth—the true cost of armor.

**Gayle Bryan**

The True Cost of Armor

1996, 44³/₄" x 38³/₄"
Bellevue, Washington

### *Erika Carter*

#### Journey

1995, 66" x 46"
Bellevue, Washington

*Journey* continues my work addressing personal progress. Choosing a path as a metaphor for life's journey, I painted fabrics for the path with circular strokes, reminiscent of the annual growth rings that mark the age of a tree. By abstracting the path in the upper left corner and portraying the lower path more realistically, I suggest that whether we are traveling up the path toward the unknown future or coming down the path away from the place memories break apart and become fragmented, we live in the present.

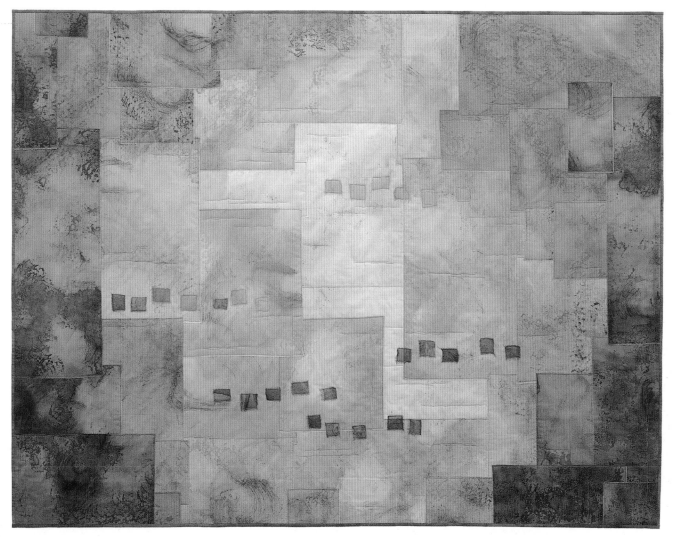

This piece continues my series of cave imagery. This imagery is both filled with time and empty of the relevance of time, creating an environment that entices the viewer to rest, contemplate, and question assumptions about time, space, and change. The horizontal rows of small, silk organza squares add to the restful quality of the environment and allude to the idea that this might be a burial place.

**Erika Carter**

Traces IV

1996, 60" x 45"
Bellevue, Washington

### *Gerry Chase*

### Repeat Block I: Neighborhood

1993, 38" x 55"
Seattle, Washington
Collection of Kaiser
Foundation Hospital

During a trip to Norway and Sweden I photographed architectural elements and landscape textures, which I later transferred to fabric for use in *Repeat Block I: Neighborhood.* I repeated the house motif in a nontraditional way and used the transfers to suggest a relationship between the actual architectural details and the archetypal meaning of neighborhood.

While my methods vary, I often create a "canvas" by using fabric and thread as well as conventional quilt-top construction techniques, and then I apply pastels or acrylic paints directly to the cloth. To a certain extent in my work, the *quilt* is subject matter. I am drawn to repetition. I am also attracted to various forms of the *container* or the *vessel* as subject matter.

**Gerry Chase**

Nine-Patch II: Cups

1996, 24" x 25"
Seattle, Washington

### *Gerry Chase*
## Repeat Block II: Six Bowls

1996, 40" x 29"
Seattle, Washington

For this piece, I used conventions of the American quiltmaking tradition, including Log Cabin piecing and appliqué, and made the border an active part of the composition. I particularly love the repeat-block format for its invitation to express difference within sameness.

Postage stamps, which provide arrays of multiple images and an abundance of borders and text, are a rich source of inspiration for me. I find the combination of sampler and repeat-block formats irresistible for its ability to show sameness within difference and difference within sameness. This piece reflects my penchant for making the border an active part of my compositions and for using text for its visual characteristics.

**Gerry Chase**

Repeat Block IV: Four Vessels

1996, 29" x 25"
Seattle, Washington

### *Janice Coffey*

#### Annie Bananie at Bow Lake

1996, 58" x 64"
Bellingham, Washington

*Annie Bananie at Bow Lake* is about my friend Ann Strout, who died last year. Her life was filled with love, energy, interest, and accomplishment. Ann was generous and tolerant. She had a sense of fun to a degree I have never seen in anyone else. I love and miss her.

Photo by Hazel Ayre Hynds

The richly colored reddish trunk of the Pacific madrona is particularly beautiful when set among the deep green vegetation surrounding Puget Sound. I find the smoothly peeled trunks emerging from mossy undergrowth irresistible, and I especially love them against the deep green waters of the Sound.

Visualizing tree trunks as Nature's most spectacular use of fiber, it may seem a bit naive to try to evoke this with the delicacy of cloth. But some hand-dyed fabrics are so rich in depth and texture that we can pretend we are touching the tree bark while we slip with our souls into the scene.

Judy Robertson hand-dyed many of the fabrics used in this piece.

## Joan Colvin

### Madrona in Cove

1996, 41" x 57"
Bow, Washington
Collection of Richard and Evadna Lynn

**_Joan Colvin_**

Heron in Reeds

1995, 50" x 54½"
Bow, Washington
Collection of Cindy Tims
and Steve Skelton

When I continuously explore a subject, for instance, the spirit and configuration of the heron, it's a great triumph when "heron leg" fabric leaps out at me! If I have the legs, they can go anywhere. In this case, the legs needed a reedy, marshy setting.

My present interest in the spirit and configuration of herons leads me to see them in a variety of fabrics and settings. A piece of black-and-white fabric—feathered and leafy but quite formal—led to the concept of an old block print, which prints imperfectly and fades into various shades of brown and black. Using fabric pens to create my own heron bodies and leaves, I extended the commercial fabric into a coherent piece that evokes the somewhat embellished grandeur of the heron in the privacy of the deep woods.

### Joan Colvin

Heron Woodblock

1995, 47" x 58½"
Bow, Washington

### *Joan Colvin*

#### Woman with Madrona

1996, 42" x 47 ½"
Bow, Washington

Sometimes the subject matter chooses *me*. I'm following in a long line of visual people who couldn't resist the magic of how bodies and flowing fabrics intermingle. It's a formidable group—but I'm pulled in as they were. As I form the fabric, I'm mentally painting, drawing, and sculpting as well.

I'm always delighted by the face emerging from the fabric and what she wants me to say about her. When I begin to know, I simplify the lines and shapes, trying to keep my vision alive and active and to sense where I'm going while I'm stitching. If I leave her for long, her voice might slip away and I'd lose that moment of understanding.

No matter who we are, our breath stops for the few moments we watch swans in flight. Swans in the air are huge and loud and only sometimes graceful. Can such weighty birds truly maintain momentum and keep themselves aloft?

When we see their determined, long necks, we know they can.

I like that I have seen them. I like that other persons from ancient, mystical times have seen them too. A shared moment, quite timeless.

**Joan Colvin**

Observing Wild Swans

1996, 38½" x 57½"
Bow, Washington

Photo by Mark Frey

## Stephanie Randall Cooper

### The Approach

1994, 65" x 61"
Everett, Washington

Although not a game to those who have thought about this final change and are alert to the symptoms, the approach of menopause can be seen as an adventure—not knowing when it will begin, how the body will react, or even what one's response will be. Will the onset of menopause be a gentle announcement of changes on the way, or will it broadcast to all within sight, reluctantly persistent and invasive? Life goes along merrily, until one day it forces itself upon us, and we may or may not be ready.

I construct my work with a "cut and paste" method, cutting random shapes from fabric. I use fabric glue sparingly to attach the shapes to a base fabric or to one another. The glue holds the composition in place while I machine quilt.

Photo by Mark Frey

She is Everygirl, Everywoman. She is young, just beginning to understand what it means to be female. She's wondering about boys, friends, clothes, school, what's expected of her. She's still very much a child, but her ideas are developing as well as her body.

This soft color palette symbolizes her childlike qualities while the bolder range is indicative of her coming of age. An equal weaving of past, an anxious present, and a hopeful future.

## Stephanie Randall Cooper

### Blossom 2

1995, 60" x 40"
Everett, Washington

### *Stephanie Randall Cooper*

#### Nine Patch: Soliloquy

1996, 70" x 70"
Everett, Washington

A private conversation, an unspoken thought, and the unfettered musings of an ordinarily content-oriented person surrounded me as I dyed the cloth used in this piece. For the quilt, I chose colors randomly, those to my immediate liking, without a care as to outcome. I considered the composition's wholeness in addition to working with individual pieces, in a confluence of quilt idiom and abstract design.

This is the fourth quilt in a series based on a branch sketch. The "sketch" is a basic pattern, a rough combination of fabric shapes that enables me to see the structure of my design. I start with the same design configuration for every piece in the series. For each quilt, I first considered the shapes in the composition, then tried a variety of construction techniques. In *Winter Yellows*, the branches as well as the complex borders are pieced.

I kept to fairly neutral tones in the preceding works of this series, but a certain amount of the winter blahs made yellow seem a good choice for this piece. My mood elevated—it was pure joy working with a wall of intense, warm color.

My work often stays on the design wall for several weeks—even months—while I consider how I want to quilt it. I usually defer the quilting until all the compositional work of a series is done. Machine quilting each piece leads me to the next in the series, a progression that continually builds on my ideas and experience. So although I constructed *Winter Yellows* during the winter of 1996, I did not quilt it until the following fall.

## Cynthia Corbin

### Winter Yellows

1996, 46" x 41"
Woodinville, Washington

### *Cynthia Corbin*

### Two-Way Stretch: Shards

1995, 61" x 55"
Woodinville, Washington

This work is an exploration of shapes moving across a surface. A piece of art glass by Dale Chihuly inspired the idea of distorting a grid by pulling it in two directions at the same time yet allowing the shapes to hold some integrity. The challenge of manipulating the fabric, working toward the illusion of a more fluid, elastic form while maintaining a brittle quality, was my particular interest.

It seems a work reaches its own identity somewhere in the process of its creation. From this point, my ideas of what a work means and what my aims are,

become overshadowed by the power of the piece itself. *Two-Way Stretch: Shards* began to show signs of addressing some life issues I was ignoring. Moving recently to the Northwest (and leaving my grown children behind in California) had created a context I found uncomfortable. I was being pulled in two directions at once. In the quilt, I resolved this conflict by surrounding the chaotic center with shapes that stabilized and contained it, maybe even controlled it.

Photo by Ken Wagner

If ever I was savaged by obsession, *Threshold* was it. The piece grew of its own accord, under its own volition, into what might first be perceived as a grotesque caricature of a quilt. I saw it change under my needle, watched it warp and buckle, beyond my control. I was entranced by the effects of line upon line of intensive machine quilting that "developed" the quilt, giving it the quality of a photographic transparency laid over its surface. *Threshold's* sculptural quality makes it an awkward step forward, a step through to some other place. I have never experienced so perfect a translation of my experience into fabric. *Threshold* lets me know I am not in charge. I know the direction I want to go; I do not know what it will look like when I get there.

*Threshold* is the second in a series of quilts for which I used a collage approach. Doorways and windows and what moves in and out of them became my subject matter. The transformation of this piece began with the quilting. In order to develop the pattern I wanted, I had to stitch the lines closer and closer together. Gradually the pattern emerged, along with *Threshold's* character.

## *Cynthia Corbin*

### Threshold

1993, 53" x 59"
Woodinville, Washington

### *Cynthia Corbin*

Swing Time

1995, 32" x 40"
Woodinville, Washington

Midnight, time passing, shifts in space and in my life; having the blues, being out of bounds, filling time with a void, avoiding thought, avoiding action, avoid- ing result—these are all thought moments that swing through my mind in the early morning hours, when my mind clicks into gear and will not let me sleep. Swing time.

The power of nature frequently inspires the imagery I use. When I travel away from the city, I never miss a sunrise or a sunset. This piece captures the brilliance of clear dawn stars against a blue velvet sky. A limited color palette and a wide variety of fabrics creates an enjoyable depth and richness. Many aspects of quilting give me pleasure: concept, design, fabric selection, and machine stitching. Fabrics bring constant surprises of color and texture.

***Melody Crust***

Star Bright

1996, 60" x 60"
Kent, Washington

### *Melody Crust*

Jacks

1996, 57" x 67"
Kent, Washington

My work is always a celebration of life. Childhood not forgotten, I still play my favorite games.

I glory in brilliant hues! Color has a voice that reaches my soul. With a respect for traditional technique, crafts-manship, and design, I experiment with shape and color to create my dream.

Quiltmaking absorbs me, either in the sewing, designing, and buying of fabric, or mentally, in the daydreaming. I love working with textiles.

Sometimes it takes an outside influence to inspire me. Traveling to the Painted Hills in eastern Oregon was the perfect opportunity to observe the shape and patterns of stars in the nighttime sky. I paper-pieced this entire quilt while awaiting sunrises and sunsets.

**Melody Crust**

Endless Night

1993, 30" x 34"
Kent, Washington

**Carla DiPietro**

Fighting Back

1995, 40" x 46"
Redmond, Washington

Even when man tries to cover the Earth with asphalt and destroy her with his greed, Nature finds a way to push through and recover. *Fighting Back* is a comment on the power and strength inherent in the Earth and how Nature's ability to revive and replenish will ultimately be the salvation of humankind.

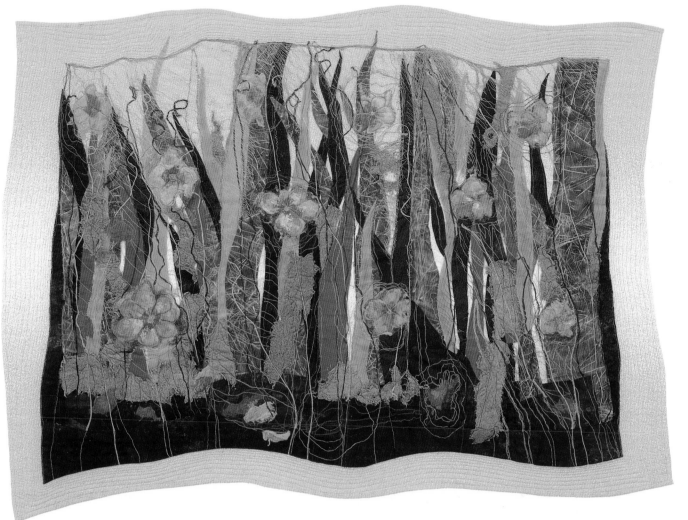

When the turmoil of the outside world seems too violent and heartbreaking, I often retreat to my beloved garden or to my studio to revitalize and renew my faith in goodness. Nature offers a haven for the quiet observance of intricate beauty, and my studio offers a place to play with various materials for the pure joy of creating. This play is my way of bringing beauty into a seemingly cruel and harsh world.

## Carla DiPietro

### Summer's Gold

1995, 53" x 39"
Redmond, Washington

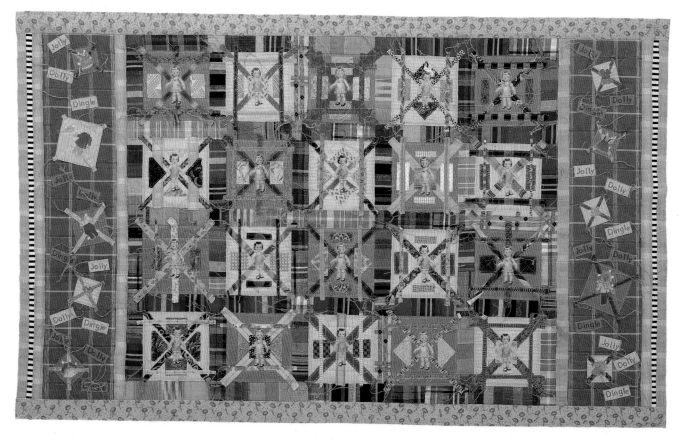

### Gretchen Echols

Jolly Dolly Dingle

1992, 72" x 48"
Seattle, Washington

*Jolly Dolly Dingle* is the second in a series featuring paper dolls from my childhood collection. The impetus for the piece came from a theme competition called "Renew, Reuse, Recycle." I reused my paper dolls in a new way and recycled unused fabric shapes from previous projects. I sought to use the quilt idiom—the repeat square set into sashing—to renew a traditional quilt set.

I also wanted to experiment with unfinished edges. Since the work is meant to hang on the wall, seams are not necessary as aspects of construction. I overlapped the fabrics and topstitched them in place. The raw edges complement the texture created by the quilting threads, which are pulled to the front and tied off, the ends left hanging. I leave all my thread ends hanging on the front of my work, which is both an aesthetic and a practical decision. Life is too short to work in all the thread ends of my pieces.

I hope viewers find *Jolly Dolly Dingle* amusing, as I do—something to bring smiles to our faces in a troubled time.

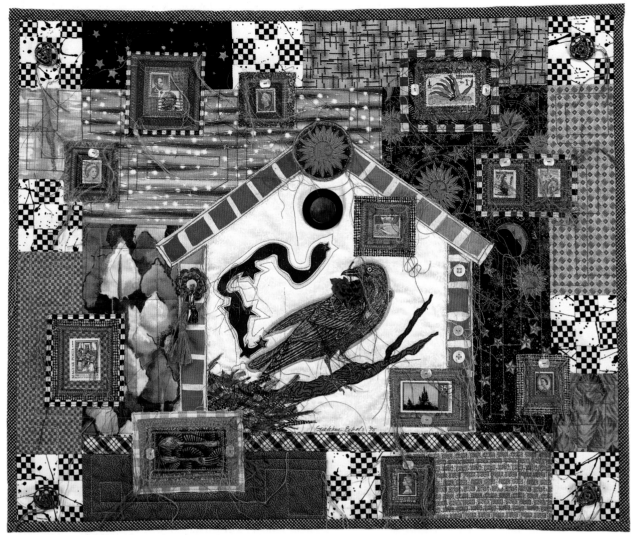

Photo by Roger Schreiber

This piece is a visual prayer to the crow spirit guide who played a major role in the creation myths of Pacific Northwest Native Americans. I used found objects (postage stamps) as memory devices for ideas I wanted to preserve in my mind. The swimmers stamp prompts me to "keep my head above water" and not sink under a sea of things to do. Franklin and Lincoln stamps together form my birth year and honor the ideals these men stood for. The printing press refers to my love of reading. Four queens at the four compass points encourage me to give my best in all areas of my life.

The woman with the mirror reminds me of the importance of the examined life. The woman carrying her sack on a stick commemorates the journey of life. The silverware represents my mother; the trees remind me to be mindful of nature and the home of my animal guide.

### Gretchen Echols

## Crow House Icon: #1 Winter

1995, 26" x 21"
Seattle, Washington

Photo by Roger Schreiber

***Gretchen Echols***

Skyscraper

1994, 23½" x 37"
Seattle, Washington
Collection of Jonathan Shannon

In my work, I present images as they appear in dreams. Dream images often seem mysterious, but they have something to tell us about our daily lives.

This work, which features a "handsome prince" paper doll from my childhood collection, comments on the archetypal young man who operates only in the sunlight of reason. The Icarus myth of ancient Greece tells of the dangers of getting too close to that hot sun. At the same time the mind is beginning to soar with the beauty of lofty thought, the wings supporting these ideas are coming loose.

This "air male" quality can be found in all of us, women and men, when we use only the gifts of the intellect without tempering them with the earthy heart. Many skeletons are buried in the city of personality; acknowledging loss grounds us in this world and connects us to our relationship with all humanity.

Photo by Roger Schreiber

My paper-doll collection is the foundation of my current series, which explores archetypal and mundane aspects of human existence. This work tells the story of Persephone and the story of the descent into womanhood that all girls must traverse. Again and again we descend into the watery depths of the feminine, where an aspect of ourselves must die so that we can be renewed and reborn to flower once more.

I present imagery in my work the way images appear in dreams. Interpretations of dream events evolve out of experience; guidebooks are not provided.

My images have multiple meanings.

In the original myth, the sun saw all that occurred between Zeus and Hades as they conspired in Persephone's abduction. In the work, the viewer sees the beautiful maiden poised assuredly in her dance, moments before she is snatched into the underworld. Simultaneously, the salmon, the Celtic symbol of wisdom, arises from the deep to initiate the girl into the woman's mystery of blood, death, and life.

Water can be a symbol of the unconscious, the underworld, and the feminine. The promise of renewal or rebirth is present in the floral growth that rises from the watery depths into the upper world.

### *Gretchen Echols*

## Innocentia Descending

1994, 23" x 30"
Seattle, Washington
Collection of Doug duMas
and Cherry Haisten

**Pia Fish**

At the Temple
of the Queen of Pineapple

1995, 47" x 18"
Seattle, Washington

Tourists visiting the Land of the Pineapple People might see these three monuments, erected to honor a benign and beloved ruler.

*Where Have All the Flowers Gone?* is one of a series in which I used one set of templates to create a variety of effects. While working on another quilt in this series, I watched Katerina Witt skate her tribute to the people of Sarajevo during the Winter Olympics. Her performance moved me to use these templates to create a similar mood of nostalgia, wistfulness, sadness, and hope.

After struggling to make the piece look the way I imagined it, I gave up and let the work create itself on the design wall. At one level, the reds and grays are representational: Katerina wore red and skated on ice. At another level, red stands for war's violence, bloodshed, and anger, while the grays evoke hopelessness, sadness, and loss. Rays of sunlight (hope for better times) shoot through the gloom. The circles create the sense of a figure skater's motion on ice.

I experimented with color, aware of how our perception of a hue changes when the colors around it change, and I played with figure and ground interchangeability. Machine quilting encourages the eye to perceive the circles as motion rather than as static shapes.

### Elizabeth Ford-Ortiz

## Where Have All the Flowers Gone?

1994, 56" x 62"
Langley, Washington

50

Photo by Roger Schreiber

### *Elizabeth Ford-Ortiz*

Over, Under, Around and Through

1994, 56" x 62"
Langley, Washington
Collection of Susan Klein
and David Berkowitz

*Over, Under, Around and Through* is another in a series in which I used the same curved- and straight-line templates to create a variety of effects. As in *Where Have All the Flowers Gone?* (page 49), I experimented with color perception and with figure and ground interchangeability. Some shapes in this quilt incorporate black-and-white geometric patterns. I used traditional piecing, experimenting with design and color rather than with surface embellishment and texture. Machine quilting encourages the eye to follow paths not evident in the piecing.

Photo by Roger Schreiber

*Hidden Light* is one of three studies I made to express my feelings about my daughter during a difficult time in her teen years. The studies were emotionally charged for me. This piece represents my feeling that my daughter's talent and potential were trapped inside her, while chaos reigned around her. My fascination with the way the properties of a color can change, depending on the surrounding colors, is an important part of all my work. Sometimes the quilting lines encourage the eye to follow certain paths; at other times they reinforce the feeling of the work.

**Elizabeth Ford-Ortiz**

Hidden Light

1995, 36" x 32"
Langley, Washington
Collection of Joanie Govedare

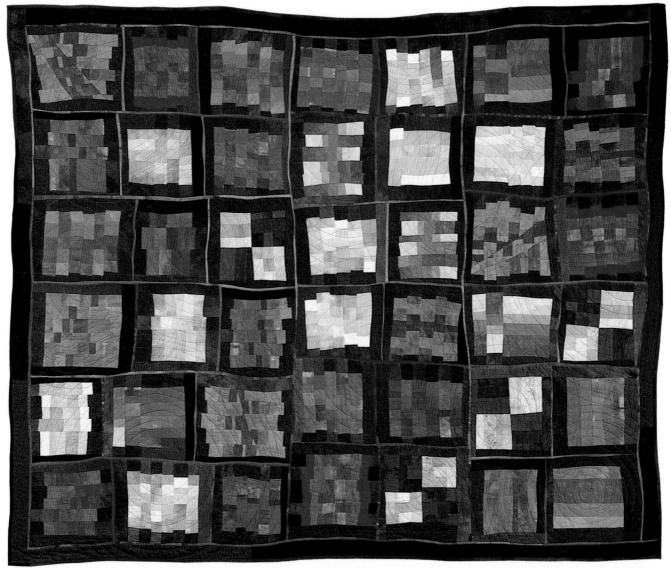

**Elizabeth Ford-Ortiz**

Take a Break #1

1995, 62" x 52"
Langley, Washington

In 1994 much of my work dealt with turmoil and stress in my life. While such work was no doubt lifesaving therapy, I felt a need to just enjoy the color and texture of fabric in my quiltmaking. So began the Take a Break series—an opportunity to play. Each square is a little composition "floating" on a dark background. The circular quilting adds a flowing dimension to the relatively angular piecing patterns.

Once, while working on a quilt, I was struck by the design possibilities of lines extending behind and through other lines and shapes. When making *Slices of Life,* I strove to create an optical illusion in which the eye could not decide what was figure and what was ground. The squares extend beyond the quilt's boundaries, reducing the sense of confinement.

**Elizabeth Ford-Ortiz**

Slices of Life

1996, 42" x 42"
Langley, Washington
Collection of Damon Arndt

**Elizabeth Ford-Ortiz**

Growing Up is Hard to Do

1995, 30" x 30"
Langley, Washington

This piece is something of a departure from my previous work. I took a class at Quilt/Surface Design Symposium entitled "Abstraction from Representation," which was taught by Arturo Alonzo Sandoval. For a number of years, I have wanted to make quilts expressing the feeling and experience of different areas of my life and relationships, and this piece is an early effort to incorporate representation into abstract work. The squares alternate two images of my daughter—one as an innocent preadolescent and one as a "rebellious" teen. I made the patterned fabric by alternating photo transfers of these images in a smaller scale.

Men in the Western Kasai region of south-central Zaire weave Kuba cloth from single, untwisted fibers of raffia. After the cloth has been woven, the women decorate it in geometric patterns, usually combining continuous-fiber and cut-pile embroidery techniques. The Kuba cloths are usually made into skirts worn by both men and women. In the fall of 1995 I purchased an antique Kuba cloth and, inspired, began a series of Kuba quilts.

I used curvilinear piecing to re-create the feel of the Kuba cloth's powerful design and to experiment with color, value, and scale. As always, placing the same color in different environments to see how it appears to change is an important aspect of my work.

**Elizabeth Ford-Ortiz**

Kuba III

1996, 50" x 42"
Langley, Washington

Photo by Mark Frey

### Nancy Forrest

## Street of Dreams

1995, 58" x 75"
Seattle, Washington
Collection of
All Star Media, Inc.

*Street of Dreams* is the second in a series of quilts about the building of dreams, my love of houses, and my dream of owning my own home.

Houses are magical entities, each with its own personality, soul, and charm. Houses are often the objects of dreams, as well as being structures that nurture us while we build our lives and pursue other dreams.

I "build" my houses spontaneously, out of many cut-fabric shapes, combining them collage-style. I know the house is ready to be sewn when it comes alive for me and I feel a sense of magic.

As I build my fabric houses, I am reminded of how we build dreams in a similar fashion—one piece at a time, with the vision always in our hearts and minds.

The Bellevue Art Museum commissioned this quilt to commemorate the fiftieth anniversary of its Arts and Crafts Fair, which is one of the largest fairs of its kind in the country.

I wanted to capture the joy and festivity of a celebration, along with a great awe for the art and artists represented at the fair. Since art is magical to me, I placed the various arts and crafts as if they were floating out of a magic fair tent. I airbrushed the fabrics to get the vibrant and gradated colors.

### Nancy Forrest

Pacific Northwest Arts and Crafts Fair Fiftieth Anniversary Quilt

1996, 53" x 65"
Seattle, Washington
Collection of The Raimondi Institute

**Maria Groat**

City Blues

1996, 30" x 49"
Bainbridge Island, Washington

This work is part of a series dealing with the blues. White Folks Blues. Morning Blues. Rent Blues. Paisley Blues. Got-them-don'tcha-mess-wit'-me-Blues!

*City Blues* is about being raised in the country and wanting to go to the city. Bright lights, nightlife, excitement. Fast cars and faster people. Sirens. Screeching tires. Smell of exhaust. Wet alleys. Blowing paper. Fences. Graffiti.

*City Blues* is about being raised in the city and wanting to go to the country.

Simple life, smell of new-mown hay, baby lambs. Daisies along the roadside. Smell of fresh air.

*City Blues* is about the diminishing countryside and the growth of the city. It's about too many people and too little space. It mourns a quiet lifestyle that will shortly be foreign to all of us.

Embellishments, loose threads, and unfinished edges symbolize the demise of one lifestyle and the questionable richness of another.

Frustrated with traditional quilting and impatient with repetition, I began to study a variety of contemporary artists. In my reading, I found most experimented with their media.

This work, an experiment in color and tessellating blocks, produced a new kind of nine patch, nontraditional and abstract. I enjoy experimenting, not knowing what will, mostly by happenstance, ultimately evolve.

**Pat Hedwall**

Improvisations I

1995, 22" x 18"
Camano Island, Washington

**Pat Hedwall**

Winter Sunrise

1996, 24" x 31"
Camano Island, Washington

There are times in winter when I wake early and look into the dark eastern sky. Everything appears blue-black—sky, mountains, and trees. As dim light starts to sharpen the outlines of the mountains, colors emerge in the sky: yellow, orange, and red. This is the moment just before the birds start to sing and the world awakens.

Sometimes it's purple and sometimes it's not.
Sometimes it's cool and sometimes it's hot.
But always down deep in its hidden landscape
Is fearful erosion and moving earth plates

That fracture and thunder down under the ground
While children lie dreaming and sleeping so sound.

We're never too certain of what will occur,
Our future is always somewhat of a blur.
But up on the surface it looks so divine
With sunshine and blue skies and weather sublime.

This small piece is an exercise in the use of yellow. I surrounded "improvisational" nine-patch blocks with other blocks made from hand-dyed fabrics.

**Pat Hedwall**

California Landscape

1995, 24" x 22"
Camano Island, Washington

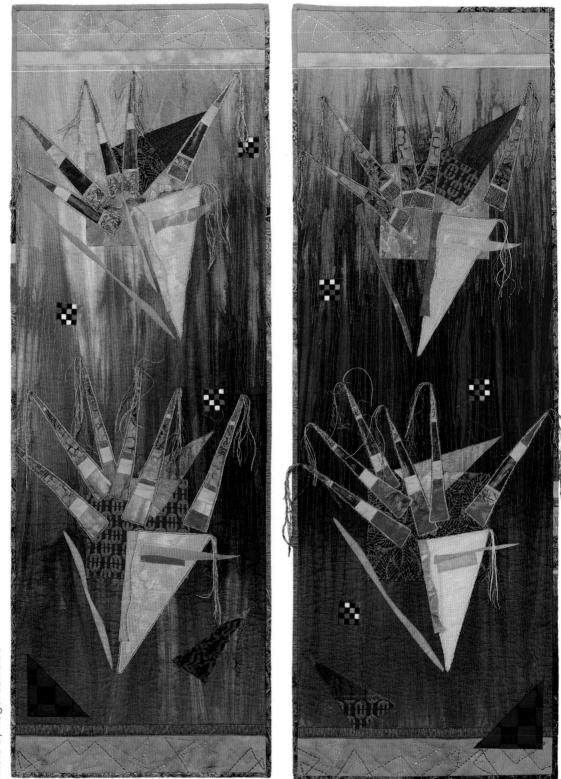

Photo by Roger Schreiber

**Elizabeth Hendricks**

Faces II

1994, 40" x 54"
Seattle, Washington

Faces emerge, as in dreams, and float—detached, half-represented, half-understood. Different emotions appear in the faces. Some have tear tracks, some are joyful, with hair flying like my friend Su's when we walked the cliffs of Whidbey Island while laughter and blowing hair teased the wind.

Photo by Roger Schreiber

I made this work in celebration of my sister Deborah's anniversary, trying to capture some of the joy, exuberance, and sense of place of her joyous wedding twenty-five years ago in Athens. This piece reflects the richness of the masculine and feminine imagery found throughout the Acropolis. Stitched within the bold Ionic and Doric columns are a caryatid and a warrior, while—with a little artistic time warp—Michelangelo's David and a fifth-century B.C. statuette of Athena stand in the pediment above. The propylaeum, or gateway, to the Acropolis floats beneath a film of hand-dyed silk. The blue of the background is like the water and sky of the Aegean.

### Elizabeth Hendricks

## Dancing at the Acropolis

1995, 39" x 51"
Seattle, Washington
Collection of Deborah and Bruce Hird

**Elizabeth Hendricks**

Broadsided

1994, 54" x 54"
Seattle, Washington

I was broadsided while driving from my studio in Seattle's Fremont District. In this piece, I tried to capture the feeling that overwhelmed me at the moment of impact—all the world broken apart, and arms and limbs, detached, are flying.

American women and children are too often the casualties of domestic violence, homelessness, alcoholism, drug abuse, mental illness, and a multitude of other social problems. They are victims of ignorance, apathy, and prejudice, and the body count rises daily.

*Hazel Ayre Hynds*

Women in Combat II

1996, 43" x 53"
Bellingham, Washington

**Joyce Keron**

Demeter

1996, 26" x 38"
Seattle, Washington

The story of Demeter, the Good Goddess, the Goddess of Harvest, demonstrates my feeling of abundance at this time in my life. Demeter, the mother of Persephone, sorry for the desolation she caused when her daughter was taken by the Lord of the Dark, restored the land to abundance when Persephone was returned. Demeter made the fields rich with fruit, flowers, and green leaves. I found fish entering my portrait of Demeter, but I don't think she would be displeased.

Photo by Roger Schreiber

It was that time of morning, at that time of year, when the sun warms what it touches, but the chill of the dawn lingers in the shadows.

*Fall Morning* is based on a photo I took at Magnuson Park in Seattle. I go for walks there with my family, and I enjoy watching as each season has its "moment" and then transitions into the next.

## Marlene Kissler

### Fall Morning

1996, 66" x 46"
Seattle, Washington

### Marlene Kissler

Flowers

1995, 26" x 30", Seattle, Washington
Collection of Frances C. Kissler

Creating new images from dissimilar commercial fabrics challenges and delights me. *Flowers* was a learning experience in depth perception, color, and realism. I based the image on a flower arrangement by Paula Pryke in *Flowers Flowers*, which was photographed by Kevin Summers, Rizzoli, New York (used with permission).

I am seeking role models to guide me into my next stage in life—the older woman. I made this piece in a large scale to give the portrait a statuesque quality and to honor this proud woman. Choosing challenging fabrics from a limited selection I had screen-printed and painted, I concentrated on making a simple and direct rendering of the figure.

## *Margaret Ann Liston*

### Monument

1995, 44" x 63"
Seattle, Washington

**Margaret Ann Liston**

Her Garden, Her Art

1996, 38" x 54"
Seattle, Washington

This quilt honors my lifelong friend Holly, who has devoted much of her creative energy to her garden. It is a heavenly garden, inspired and expressive. *Her Garden, Her Art* captures Holly surrounded by her bountiful flowers.

Although this quilt does not look like most memento mori pieces, the transience of the flowers and of the moment suggests the passage of time, of the seasons, and of life. I composed the whole quilt, including Holly's portrait, out of pieces of decorator floral chintzes and other floral fabrics.

I composed this Bacchus and his two companions out of flowers to illustrate their lighthearted spirits and their freshness in revelry and carousing. Although I wanted the piece to be joyful, the expressions of the two women suggest complex emotions beneath the surface.

When I compose people out of flowers, I am often surprised by the expressions they show. The flowers help me to be less realistic and to keep the figures loose and playful. The portraits are quirky, yet they show character.

## Margaret Ann Liston

### Bacchus and Beauties

1996, 49" x 46"
Seattle, Washington

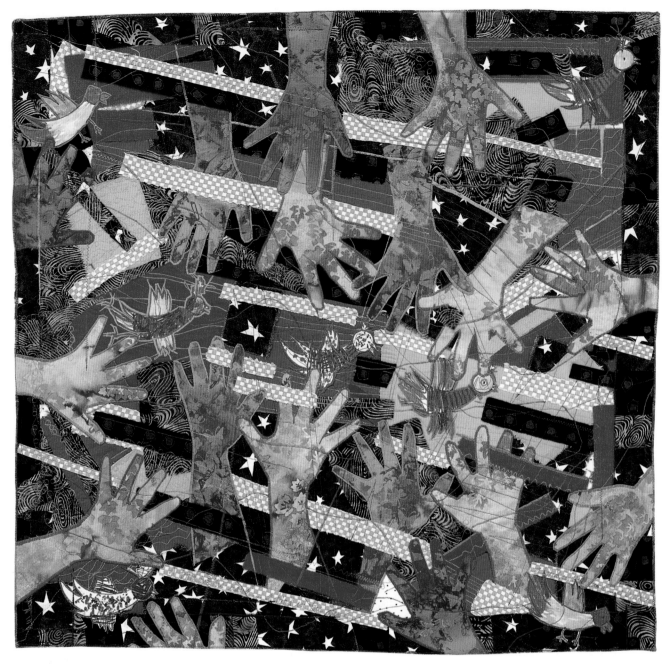

**Maude May**

A Bird in the Hand

1994, 28³/₄" x 27¹/₂"
Seattle, Washington
Collection of Jeanne Neptune

I have long been fascinated by hands. In this piece, the negative/positive shapes created by the fingers reach and interlock, touch and pull away, hold and then let go, forming intricate designs that symbolize my relationship with my daughter. She is fabric in my care, which I help to shape and form, yet she possesses her own rich pattern that I must follow. Together we create the cloth of her life.

Late at night, working in my studio
while my family sleeps, I see things...

**Maude May**

Night Visions

1995, 20½" x 17½"
Seattle, Washington

**Jamie Morgan**

Twilight

1996, 18" x 21"
Kent, Washington

What artist is not inspired by a beautiful pink-and-orange sunset? The glow of the sunlight and rising fog accentuate the abundance of colorful flowers in this imaginary garden near the forest's edge.

For much of my life, I have been locked in an adversarial, black-or-white relationship with myself and Life. In the Christian mystic tradition, there is a concept called *Godspace*, that space wherein what we perceive as dualities dwell *together*, where angels work, where miracles happen. Mystics strove to live in the Godspace by recognizing the seeming dualities that confront us, the either/or situations, and to embrace all that seems in conflict as part of a greater whole.

This quilt is dedicated to Barbara Ryan, who blessed and believed in me as I moved toward the Godspace, struggling to discover the richness of selves within me and to embrace them in wholeness.

I based the figure in this piece on Auguste Rodin's sculpture *Woman Crouching*.

### Kathleen Marie O'Hanlon

Invitation to the Godspace

1996, 35½" x 47¾"
Seattle, Washington
Collection of the Seattle University
Wismer Women's Center

## Carol Roi Olsen

Latticeworks III

1992, 65" x 54"
Bainbridge Island, Washington

This is third in a series that features a simple block that, through changes in coloration, I use to create three-dimensional effects. In the *Latticeworks III* configuration, the image is of two grids, one on top of the other. The foreground grid includes a progression of yellow through green to blue, and the underlying grid is made up of random, subdued colors. The black-to-gray background gradations add to the piece's dimensionality. While constructing this piece, I was fascinated by the sensual differences apparent in colors placed next to dark gray in one area and light gray in another.

Human sanity is frighteningly fragile. As a species and as individuals, we model our behavior on what we see around us in childhood. The gestures we learn as children become the ones we repeat as adults. Those patterns are changed only with great difficulty. When bits of the present are torn away, when the seemingly stable structures we painfully build are disturbed or distorted—whether by war, cultural change, or family dysfunction—we see through to our irretrievable, irreversible, irredeemable past.

### *Cherry Partee*

## The Judgment of Children

1991, 113" x 90"
Seattle, Washington

**Cherry Partee**

The Gift

1994, 96" x 20" x 48"
Seattle, Washington

This work is about undervaluing and overlooking. When exhibiting *The Gift*, I try to choose a site somewhat out of the light or in an inconspicuous place. While conceiving and working on this piece, I was thinking of what people do to themselves and to others, as well as about the place of needlework in the art world.

At this work's first exhibition, a lot of care was taken with security. Flat quilts were bolted to the wall, and all staff were notified that my work was unusual and could not be secured. The second night, a member of the maintenance crew—first night on the job—put the entire work into the trash compactor. Literally, it was not recognized as art.

Everyone was horrified. I was delighted. The incident perfectly underlined the meaning of the piece, which had become a performance. I begged for cleaning rags from the exhibition space and stenciled them with the words "THIS IS NOT ART—THIS IS TRASH" and "NOT ART—TRASH." I re-created the whole piece, incorporating the cleaning rags into the new quilt.

Velvet ropes were placed in front of the re-created work. I set the ropes aside every time I went to see the show. Nobody won this quiet, genteel battle of wills, which raised questions for me: For whom is art made? Who should control its presentation?

On at least five randomly chosen occasions during the exhibition of this piece, I choose one person, also at random, and approach them, saying, "I have a gift for you if you want it." The person says yes or no. If the answer is yes, I open the boxes, and one by one, like petals revealing the heart of a flower, I unfold the quilts and lay them out flat. "Choose the one you would like to keep." The person chooses, takes the gift, and leaves. I refold the other quilts, replacing the one taken away, and return them to the boxes. I close and stack the boxes for the next time.

I hear much discussion about the role of art in life. Criticism has focused on the gallery system, the commercialization of our spiritual life, and art as an activity separate from everyday life. Art that "makes people think" or engages the viewer only intellectually is favored by some as a protest against art as empty aesthetics, thought to be naturally aligned with an oppressive authority. On the other hand, art of a purely aesthetic nature is favored by others because of its beauty; physical appeal; and positive, unprovoking, consoling nature. The fact that ideas of beauty are wildly variable seems to go unnoticed. Both extremes insist that neither view is compatible with the other. In my opinion aesthetics (which encompasses all tastes, and is not the same thing as beauty), intellect, and meaning are inseparable.

This work is a combination of object and performance, designed to incorporate beauty, meaning, and intellect. It uses the beautiful; it acts out meaning; and it creates and comments upon the relationship between high art and low, contained self-reference, and public interaction. Profligate in giving, cautious of selling, it creates a multiplicity of implied, reconciled opposites.

**Cherry Partee**

The Rain Falls on the Just and the Unjust

1993, 60" x 36" x 60"
Seattle, Washington

Photo by Mark Frey

### *Karen Perrine*

Forest Flowing

1992, 138" x 76"
Tacoma, Washington
Collection of John Walsh III

*Forest Flowing* is a simple arrangement of large rectangles and triangles cut from intensely patterned and colored hand-painted fabric. Half the design is in the realm of air; half is in water. The two realms have little contact, only the rocks are at home in each. The scene is intimate, yet the scale is large.

The forest is a dynamic, busy, mysterious place. Imagine the trails and hollows that might exist behind the outer facade.

Photo by Sharon Risedorph

A willow sapling that has sprouted rather precariously—nearly in the water and in the shadow of a huge boulder— bends toward the light. Decades from now (if the little tree survives), the willow will have pushed the boulder aside.

**Karen Perrine**

Slender Purchase

1995, 32" x 53"
Tacoma, Washington
Collection of Gordon and Joan Stavig

### *Karen Perrine*

Red Forest

1991, 71" x 49"
Tacoma, Washington

I have conversations with myself about duality, a state that seems clearly evident in natural cycles. Creating fictional landscapes seems a perfectly reasonable thing to do while conversing this way.

I grew up in a rural area and spent a lot of time as a child watching the effects of the wind, reflections on water, and the budding and dying that mark the seasons. My nature-inspired works reflect past influences as well as current ideas. I'm particularly interested in water and all its dual states: transparent/opaque, liquid/solid, life-giving/life-taking. I'm curious about the intersection of rock and water, one element so solid, the other so seemingly ephemeral; yet eventually water carves and pounds rock to sand—a metaphor for perseverance, patience, and fortitude.

In *Red Forest*, the design flows all the way around two quilted garments, creating a larger scene by overlapping. The garments are functional, yet they create a flat landscape on a wall.

This piece originated with two thoughts: first, that a shape might contain an environment, rather than the conventional idea of an environment containing a shape, and second, that the view we have of the "outside" is dependent on characteristics of the window we are looking through. To see more of *this* view, more garments must be added.

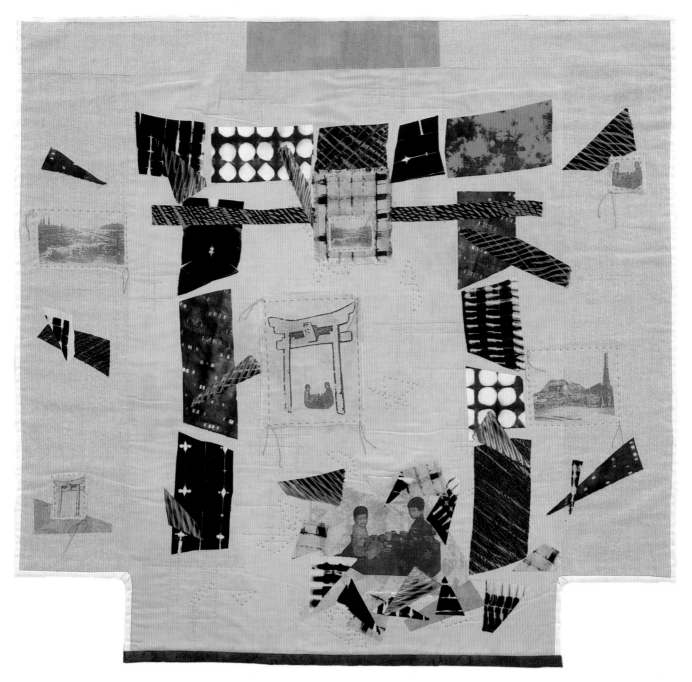

*Tori Gate* is a statement about war, destruction, and hope. It is also my tribute to my father, Steven Fuller. The images are drawn from a series of slides taken by my father, an infantry officer, in Nagasaki. It was two weeks after the United States detonated an atomic bomb there in August 1945. In the most ironic and compelling image, a tori gate, the Shinto symbol of the gateway to heaven, is the only structure that remains standing in the blast area. The photo of the little boy and girl having a tea ceremony with odds and ends of dishes was taken on the porch of their destroyed home.

The back of the quilt echoes the front, in the Japanese tradition of finishing all surfaces of an object. The shape of the quilt is reminiscent of a ceremonial kimono. I bound the piece in white, the Japanese color of mourning.

## *Marise Fuller Person*

Tori Gate

1996, 61" x 59"
Olympia, Washington

**Jill Pollard**

The Fire of 10,000 Stars Burns
Within Her

1994, 20" x 32" x 8"
Roy, Washington
Collection of Jeannette Iverson
and Brett Trowbridge

Constructing and discovering changes in relationship, in my work and in me, makes the discovery of "what it means" more exciting than formal considerations. However, only through successful design do I initially interest a viewer, inviting closer inspection and discovery of what one can know only through close contact.

Each piece's story emerges as I work. Sometimes I think I know what I'm doing when I begin, but the reason I do the work is to learn the story. My participation in the process is only one of the elements necessary to allow small pieces of the Mystery to manifest in physical form. The works function as bridges—a means of establishing relationships and making connections.

My soft sculptures grew out of the human imagery in my quilted hangings. Not content to remain trapped in two dimensions, the bodies "asked" to be fully formed, and then took on a life of their own, their many pieces and varied postures reflecting the complexity of life. Presented naked and without a face, each "doll" demands that I look for her essence and not at her facade. Her mood changes with each incarnation— playful, pensive, angry, reverent—but something about her endures. She has many stories to tell.

Aphra Behn was a truly remarkable seventeenth-century poet, whose unconventional and varied career included spying for Charles I and being sent to debtor's prison. After her release, she became the first English woman in history to support herself by writing. My coat is named in her honor; I like to imagine her wearing it.

**Donna Prichard**

*Aphra's Coat*

1995, 52" x 57"
Bellevue, Washington

**Donna Prichard**

Morgaine's Coat III

1994, 55" x 56"
Bellevue, Washington
Collection of Edmonds
Arts Festival Museum

I named the first coat of this series for Merlin, the next three for King Arthur's half-sister. I brought various dissimilar fabrics together into strips by layering, stitching, cutting, distressing, and painting. The mundane transforms into the magical: Arthurian power dressing.

Photo by Ken Wagner

This is part of a series I made to commemorate my trip to Portugal. Lamego is a town in the mountains, and the surrounding area is mainly wine country. The Lamego cemetery sits on a rise. When I was there, it was cold and gray; I wanted to capture that feeling.

*Toot Reid*

Lamego

1995, 77½" x 69½"
Tacoma, Washington

Photo by Ken Wagner

**Toot Reid**

Caminha

1995, 45½" x 67"
Tacoma, Washington

It was warm and sunny while I was in Caminha, a coastal town in Portugal that sports brightly painted fishing boats. As in many of Portugal's towns, the Caminha cemetery sits on a rise.

As a quilt teacher, I have seen the way many quilters relate to their work. Regardless of the level of expertise, each quilter has a specific area of quilting in which he or she feels competent—a comfort zone. On the other hand, every quilter has an area that is more of a stretch or challenge.

As a quilter, I alternate between these two extremes. I reach for the seemingly unattainable, return to the familiar and dear for comfort, and then stretch again.

In *Women and Their Quilts*, the quilter on the right clings to her comfort zone. The quilter on the left abandons her comfort zone to reach as far as she can. I don't know if she'll grasp her goal or fall on her face. It's the exhilaration of the reach that matters.

## Mia Rozmyn

### Women and Their Quilts

1995, 55" x 65"
Seattle, Washington

Photo by Bill Bachhuber

### *Sally A. Sellers*

#### HomeBody

1992, 59" x 56"
Vancouver, Washington
Collection of Skagit Valley
College (WSAC)

*HomeBody* is the first in my series of house quilts. The house image emerged during a difficult time in my life; my seven-year-old daughter, who has Rett syndrome, manifested medical problems so severe that I could no longer care for her in my home. To have her move to another dwelling (the children's nursing hospital) violated my maternal instinct at the deepest level. It forced me to confront such issues as the definition of love, the role of chance and fate, the role of a mother, and most painfully, what we can and cannot protect our children from, however strong our Home. A small milagro in the "doorway" of the House/Woman, is in the image of a little girl.

Photo by Bill Bachhuber

I am fascinated by house shapes and the elemental geometry involved in their representation. *TownHouse* explores these shapes through repetition and variation. The larger house shape is composed of smaller units, just as a town is a composite of buildings. The appeal of making this piece lies in enjoying the oddity of each individual home.

**Sally A. Sellers**

TownHouse

1995, 21½" x 31"
Vancouver, Washington
Collection of Samara Gilroy Hicks

Photo by Bill Bachhuber

### Sally A. Sellers

#### Not Visibly Tearful

1995, 21" x 30"
Vancouver, Washington
Collection of Elaine Anne Spence

*Not Visibly Tearful* testifies to the pain we can carry without others being aware of it. The self (here, the image of a house) can be seething with turmoil, but what is presented to the world is a decorative but fragile exoskeleton.

*Firstborn* is about the possibilities implicit at birth and the role of fate in achieving our individual destiny. The work resembles a calendar, but not one that can be interpreted. Genetics, chance, experience—all shape the passage of time. The future exists, but in indecipherable symbols.

**Sally A. Sellers**

Firstborn

1994, 32½" x 54½"
Vancouver, Washington

Photo by Bill Bachhuber

**Sally A. Sellers**

Goodnight Alice

1993, 42" x 59"
Vancouver, Washington
Collection of Alice Sellers-Subocz

I made *Goodnight Alice* for busy little girls who have a hard time letting go of the day and trusting in the restorative power of sleep.

*Flapdoodle* means "nonsense." I had fun with this piece. I exploded traditional quilt blocks with jewels and three-dimensional stars.

**Terri Shinn**

Flapdoodle

1995, 46" x 46"
Snohomish, Washington

Photo by Roger Schreiber

### Karen N. Soma

Midnight Passage

1994, 30" x 36"
Seattle, Washington

In this quilt, I wanted to explore crossing the threshold from wakefulness to sleep, conscious to subconscious, what's known to what's hidden. I visualize this path moving through darkness and shadows, blue and silver suggesting deep night lit by the moon—a time of dreams. The window image in the center is a metaphor for dreams, elusive beckonings from the soul's center. This piece can be read as a timeline: past, present, and future. It suggests the answers sought in the present have a solid base in personal history, and the two inevitably lead to the future. I wanted this work to invite quiet contemplation. Just as the silence of midnight is conducive to sleep, the stillness of the soul invites the surfacing of knowledge, balance, and peace.

Photo by Roger Schreiber

This composition's cross form has a spiritual resonance for me beyond the obvious religious symbolism. I use it as a simple icon for the human figure. The title of this piece refers to a blessed state in which the internal and the external are in balance. With all the pressures we must endure from the outside world, a basic dilemma of humanity is how to maintain the integrity of our core, protect the essence of who we are, while maintaining our connections and fulfilling our obligations to society. The issue here is an effective boundary, represented by a thin red line separating the cross/figure from the outside. Like the skin separating our body from its environment, we need a spiritual boundary to protect what is unique and precious in our souls. And like skin, this boundary functions best when thin and permeable—able to allow selective passage across its borders.

### Karen N. Soma

State of Grace

1994, 31½" x 46½"
Seattle, Washington

### Karen N. Soma

Emergence

1996, 18" x 18"
Seattle, Washington

This work is one of ten units that makes up the Contemporary QuiltArt Association's tenth-anniversary commemorative series quilt.

"Behind every great man is a woman" used to be high praise for and acknowledgment of women's traditional supportive role. I started thinking about the many roles that stand between women and their creative core—those patterns of behavior we welcome and those we resist or perhaps tolerate.

In this piece, composed of symbolic shapes, a spiral core of creative energy is covered by another, barely visible pattern; now protected from intrusive prohibitions; now emerging from behind yet another mask to join and be supported by an ongoing stream of others with a similar purpose and direction. The soul has found its family—its name is CQA.

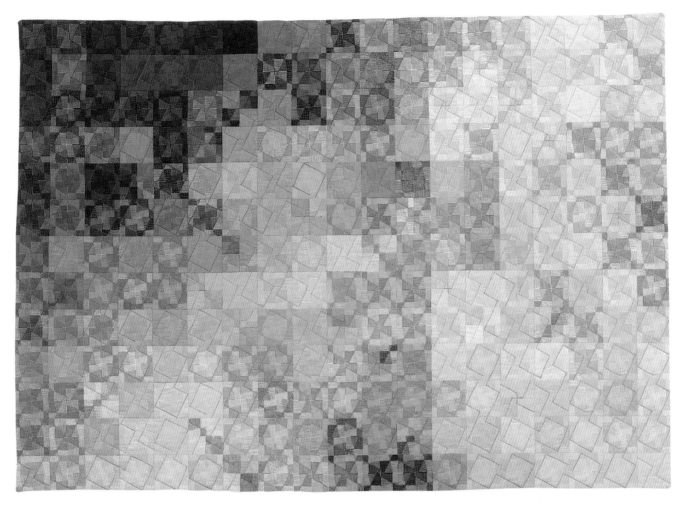

I silk-screened the cloth for this quilt, repeating one design in two different but related patterns—to my mind, they formed Xs and Os. I liked what happened when I combined the patterns in various ways, and I wanted to explore how color would alter and excite the picture. Those Xs and Os stirred thoughts of stars and voids in space, connecting with my love of the transition times of day: sunrise and sunset.

In *Solar Palette*, the delicate colors of sunrise are on the right (east), with the intense hues of sunset on the left (west). A line runs vertically through the right third of the quilt, separating the promise of dawn from dusk's fulfillment.

I wanted pattern to guide the viewer's eye across the picture plane and color to move the eye into a depth of field and back out. This combination of strong pattern and color, used as equal elements, gives the composition a pulsating intensity. My aim was to express how compelling the interplay of sun and atmosphere can be, and how transitory—the patterns shift and change before our eyes. In sunsets, as in life, nothing is certain but change, but nothing deeply felt is ever lost.

**Karen N. Soma**

Solar Palette

1992, 75" x 52"
Seattle, Washington

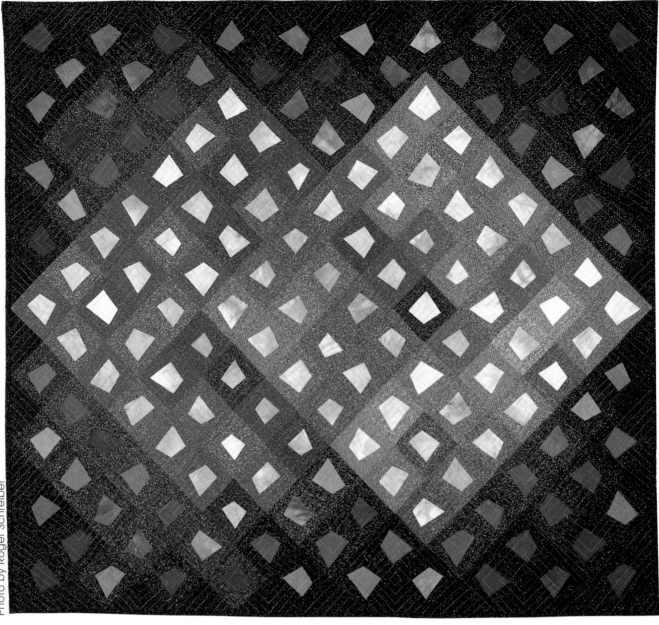

Photo by Roger Schreiber

### *Janet Steadman*

#### Return Engagement

1996, 49" x 45"
Clinton, Washington

*Return Engagement* is my response to the Pointillist Palette fabric contest. Using only the limited fabrics available on the island where I live was a challenge. For the design, I chose an overlapping diamond that is part of my latest series.

Pointillist Palette fabric strips surround hand-dyed centers in the simple on-point Log Cabin blocks.

I thought I had completed a group of quilts bearing theatrical names, only to find I had a *Return Engagement*.

As I sketched a design I had used for a previous quilt, the design distorted and gave the impression of being warped. The diamond grid skewed into a web of italic forms.

I drew the completed design onto canvas first, then machine appliquéd pieces of fabric onto the canvas to make the quilt top. The diamonds appear to float on a dark background, overlapping to create an illusion of transparency.

### Janet Steadman

Warp

1995, 43" x 34"
Clinton, Washington

### *Janet Steadman*

Wind-Blown Blaze

1996, 55" x 49"
Clinton, Washington

On a stormy winter night, my neighbors' house became engulfed in flames within minutes of a smoke-alarm warning. When the flames broke through the roof, I was forced to evacuate my own home. I ran into my studio to collect quilts.

*Wind-Blown Blaze* depicts the view from my studio window as the flames broke through my neighbors' blue metal roof and rose toward the night sky. My house was saved, but other neighbors were not as fortunate.

For six months—after fire had destroyed two neighbors' homes and nearly destroyed mine too—I looked out my studio window at a residue of ashes. This quilt was to be called "Ashes" and was to depict the colors of the ashes and rusted bits of metal. As the piece grew and the fright of the fire faded, the quilt became *Applause*, a joyous experience.

### Janet Steadman

Applause

1996, 60" x 50"
Clinton, Washington

**Laura Stocker**

Passages

1994, 25" x 21"
Seattle, Washington
Private collection

Arches, windows, and doorways have fascinated me for the last few years. As my son, Cavin, graduates from high school, I consider the passages he will be choosing throughout his life. For Cavin, the future is mysterious and magical, but he will always choose his passages with the past in mind.

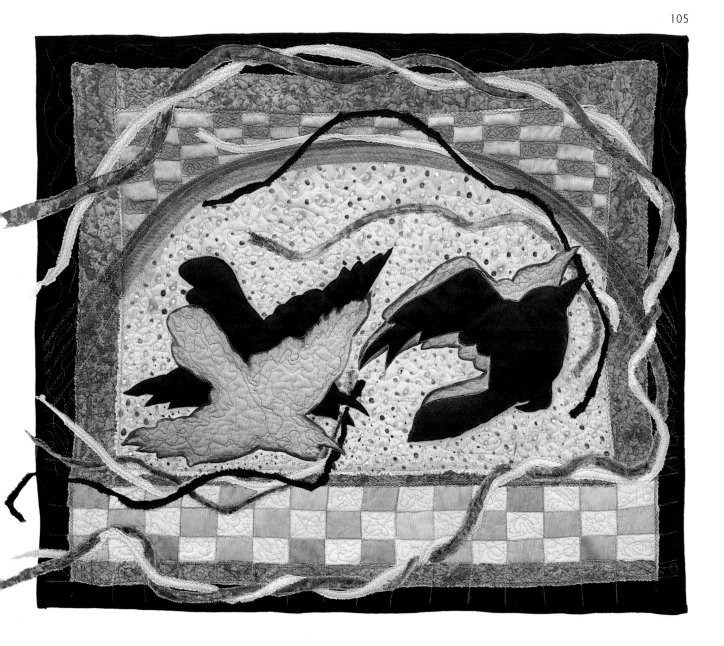

The spring equinox is a time of wind and change. It is the halfway point between winter and summer, when the day divides equally between dark and light. "Spring Allegro" from Vivaldi's *Four Seasons* inspired the rhythm of movement and color in this piece.

**Eileen Warr-Marti**

Spring Equinox—Time of Wind

1994, 33" x 28"
Seattle, Washington

**_Lorraine Torrence_**

Roadmap to the Rainbow

1993
Seattle, Washington

_Roadmap to the Rainbow_ is a four-part wearable-art ensemble that includes a coat, pants, blouse, and vest. I designed and made the garments for the 1993 American Quilter's Society fashion show and competition. The ensemble won an Honorable Mention.

For the coat, I chose a McCall's pattern, which I modified to create areas for embellishment. On the black background only, I machine echo-quilted around the appliqués, spacing the lines ³/₈" apart. For the lining, I paper-pieced five-pointed stars of brightly colored silk charmeuse into the black taffeta background.

On the vest, multicolored ¹/₂" squares mark the intersections of the diagonal grid of ¹/₂"-wide white lines. On the vest back,

the grid breaks into an asymmetrical design. I hand appliquéd five-pointed red, yellow, and blue stars over the piecing and outlined them with couched white embroidery thread. For the off-white blouse, I used multicolored silk-charmeuse–covered buttons.

### Lindi Wood

Insomnia

1993, 39" x 30"
Seattle, Washington

*Insomnia* addresses the dynamic between the wondrous serenity of wakefulness on a summer night and the frustration of coping with a lack of sleep. For years, I suffered from insomnia two to five nights a week. I saw it as both a blessing and a curse. Because of my sleeplessness, I enjoyed the solitude I craved and was denied during the day. Because of its regularity, however, I sometimes paid with frayed nerves and a disoriented mind. I addressed this dichotomy in my quilt.

# EXHIBITION BIOGRAPHY

Seafirst Gallery
Seattle, Washington
*Quilts in Reformation*
October 23–December 12, 1997

Gilmartin Gallery
University Unitarian Church
Seattle, Washington
*Reflections*
September 6–October 4, 1997

Museum of the American Quilter's
Society
Paducah, Kentucky
*On the Edge: Northwest
QuiltArt*
May 31–September 6, 1997

Gilmartin Gallery
University Unitarian Church
Seattle, Washington
*Illuminations*
February 1–28, 1997

Seattle Pacific University Gallery
Seattle, Washington
*Quilts at the Art Center*
July 21–August 28, 1996

Mesolini & Amici
Seattle, Washington
*Spur of the Moment*
April 4–May 29, 1996

Port Angeles Fine Arts Center
Port Angeles, Washington
*The Contemporary Quilt*
January 28–March 10, 1996

American Museum of Quilts and Textiles
San Jose, California
*Non-Stop Northwest*
September 8–November 4, 1995

Bellevue Art Museum
Bellevue, Washington
*Northwest Art Quilts*
February 10–April 16, 1995

Washington State Convention
and Trade Center
Seattle, Washington
*New Work: Makers, Methods,
Meanings*
September 6–December 28,
1994

Confluence Gallery
Twisp, Washington
*Private Altitude*
(three-stop tour)
October 22–November 20, 1994

Nordic Heritage Museum
Seattle, Washington
*Private Altitude*
(three-stop tour)
June 9–August 29, 1994

Tacoma Little Theater
Tacoma, Washington
*Private Altitude* (three-stop
tour)
April 20–May 20, 1994

Detail of *Observing Wild Swans*
by Joan Colvin

Seattle Pacific University
Seattle, Washington
*Difference: Fuel for Creation,
a Symposium*
October 22–23, 1993

Seattle Pacific University Gallery
Seattle, Washington
*The Difference Project*
October 20–November 20, 1993

Lynnwood Library
Lynnwood, Washington
April 6–May 4, 1993

Washington Center for Performing Arts
Olympia, Washington
*The Art of the Quilt*
January 13–February 17, 1993

Edmonds Art Festival Gallery
and Edmonds Library
Edmonds, Washington
September 1–30, 1992

Annie Wright School Gallery
Tacoma, Washington
March–April, 1992

Tri-Cities Quilt Show
Richland, Washington
April 1992

Folklife Festival
Seattle, Washington
*By Design: The Quilt as Art*
May 23–June 9, 1991

New Pieces Gallery
Berkeley, California
November 1990

In The Beginning Fabrics
Seattle, Washington
January 15–February 18, 1990

Foster/White Gallery
Seattle, Washington
*Piece by Piece: Contemporary
Quilts*
March 7–April 9, 1989

A Contemporary Theater
Seattle, Washington
September 22–October 16, 1988

Gutcheon Patchwork Gallery
New York, New York
October 1988

Edmonds Art Festival Gallery
Edmonds, Washington
*Contemporary Quilts*
October 2–30, 1987

Detail of *Street of Dreams*
by Nancy Forrest

# INDEX

Detail of *Broadsided* by Elizabeth Hendricks

# SELECTED TITLES FROM FIBER STUDIO PRESS AND THAT PATCHWORK PLACE

**FIBER STUDIO** PRESS

*Complex Cloth: A Comprehensive Guide to Surface Design*
Jane Dunnewold

*Erika Carter: Personal Imagery in Art Quilts* • Erika Carter

*Inspiration Odyssey: A Journey of Self-Expression in Quilts*
Diana Swim Wessel

*The Nature of Design* • Joan Colvin

*Thread Magic: The Enchanted World of Ellen Anne Eddy*
Ellen Anne Eddy

*Velda Newman: A Painter's Approach to Quilt Design*
Velda Newman with Christine Barnes

*Appliqué in Bloom* • Gabrielle Swain

*Bargello Quilts* • Marge Edie

*Blockbender Quilts* • Margaret J. Miller

*Color: The Quilter's Guide* • Christine Barnes

*Colourwash Quilts* • Deirdre Amsden

*Freedom in Design* • Mia Rozmyn

*Quilted Sea Tapestries* • Ginny Eckley

*Quilts from Nature* • Joan Colvin

*Watercolor Impressions* • Pat Magaret & Donna Slusser

*Watercolor Quilts* • Pat Magaret & Donna Slusser

Many titles are available at your local quilt shop or where fine books are sold. For more information, write for a free color catalog to That Patchwork Place, Inc., PO Box 118, Bothell, WA 98041-0118 USA.

U.S. and Canada, call 1-800-426-3126 for the name and location of the quilt shop nearest you.
Int'l: 1-425-483-3313 • Fax: 1-425-486-7596
E-mail: info@patchwork.com
Web: www.patchwork.com